Black-necked Stilt

Green Vegetable Bug

Steller's Jay

Snow Bunting

Northern Shrike

Blue Crab

Lobster

Prothonotary Warbler

Arctic Tern

Black-capped Mockingthrush

Brewer's Sparrow

Field Cricket

Blue Jay

Fork-tailed Storm-petrel

Elegant Tinamou

Bronze-winged Jacana

Streaked Bitt

Hawfinch

California Thrasher

Anna's Hummingbird

Yellow-billed Cuckoo

Long-tailed Tailorbird

Booted Warbl

Common Murre

Turkey

Chipping Sparrow

Green Lacewing

Atlantic Salmon

Red-winged Blackbird

Glossy Ibis

Ladybird Beetle

Golden-crowned Kinglet

Paradise Crow

Cactus Wren

Boat-tailed Grackle

Scarlet Tanager

Leopard Frog

Herring Gull

Townsend's Solitaire

Hepatic Tanager

Harlequin Bug

Evening Grosbeak

Kirtland's Warbler

Emperor Penguin

Passion Vine Butterfly

Black Vulture

Little Blue Heron

Dogfish

Chukar

Thick-billed Warbler

Paradise Riflebird

Gray Catbird

Sooty Tern

Bushy-crested Jay

Yellowhammer

American Robin

Green Iguana

Black-naped Oriole

Katydid

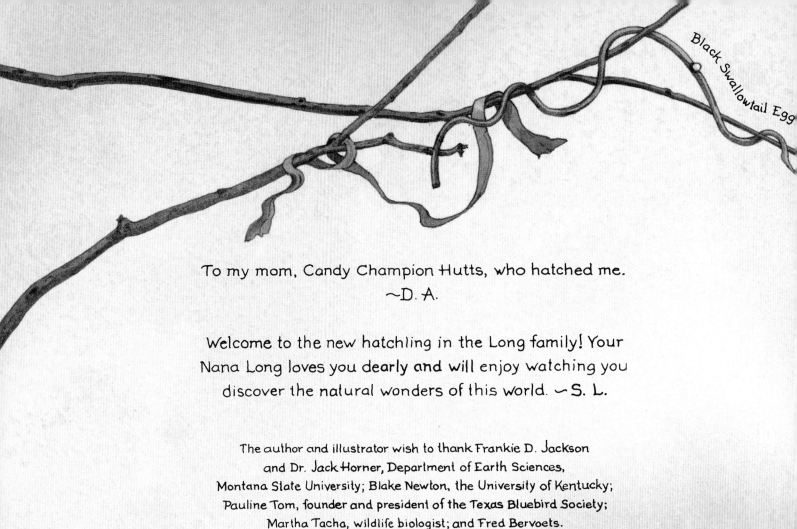

Black Swallowtail Egg

To my mom, Candy Champion Hutts, who hatched me.
~D. A.

Welcome to the new hatchling in the Long family! Your
Nana Long loves you dearly and will enjoy watching you
discover the natural wonders of this world. ~S. L.

The author and illustrator wish to thank Frankie D. Jackson
and Dr. Jack Horner, Department of Earth Sciences,
Montana State University; Blake Newton, the University of Kentucky;
Pauline Tom, founder and president of the Texas Bluebird Society;
Martha Tacha, wildlife biologist; and Fred Bervoets.

Text © 2006 by Dianna Aston.
Illustrations © 2006 by Sylvia Long.

Book design by Sara Gillingham.
Handlettered by Anne Robin and Sylvia Long.
The illustrations in this book were rendered in ink and watercolor.
Manufactured in China.

Library of Congress Cataloging-in-Publication Data
Aston, Dianna Hutts.
An egg is quiet / by Dianna Aston; illustrated by Sylvia Long.
p. cm.
ISBN-13: 978-0-8118-4428-4 (13-digit)
ISBN-10: 0-8118-4428-5 (10-digit)
1. Embryology—Juvenile literature. 2. Eggs—Juvenile literature.
I. Long, Sylvia, ill. II. Title.
QL956.5.A88 2006
591.4'68—dc22
2005012090

10 9 8 7 6 5

Chronicle Books LLC
680 Second Street, San Francisco, California 94107

www.chroniclebooks.com

Black Swallowtail

An Egg Is Quiet

by Dianna Aston ~ illustrated by Sylvia Long

chronicle books · san francisco

Black-necked Stilt

An egg is quiet.

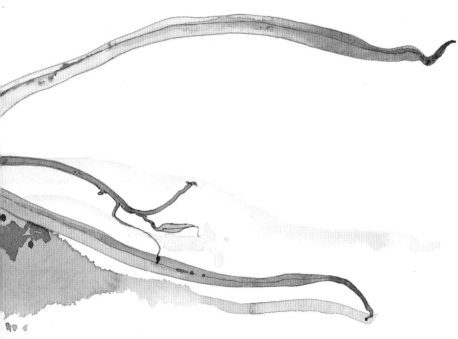

It sits there, under its mother's feathers . . .

Anna's Hummingbird

on top of its father's feet . . .

Emperor Penguin

Kemp's Ridley Sea Turtle

buried beneath
the sand.

Warm. Cozy.

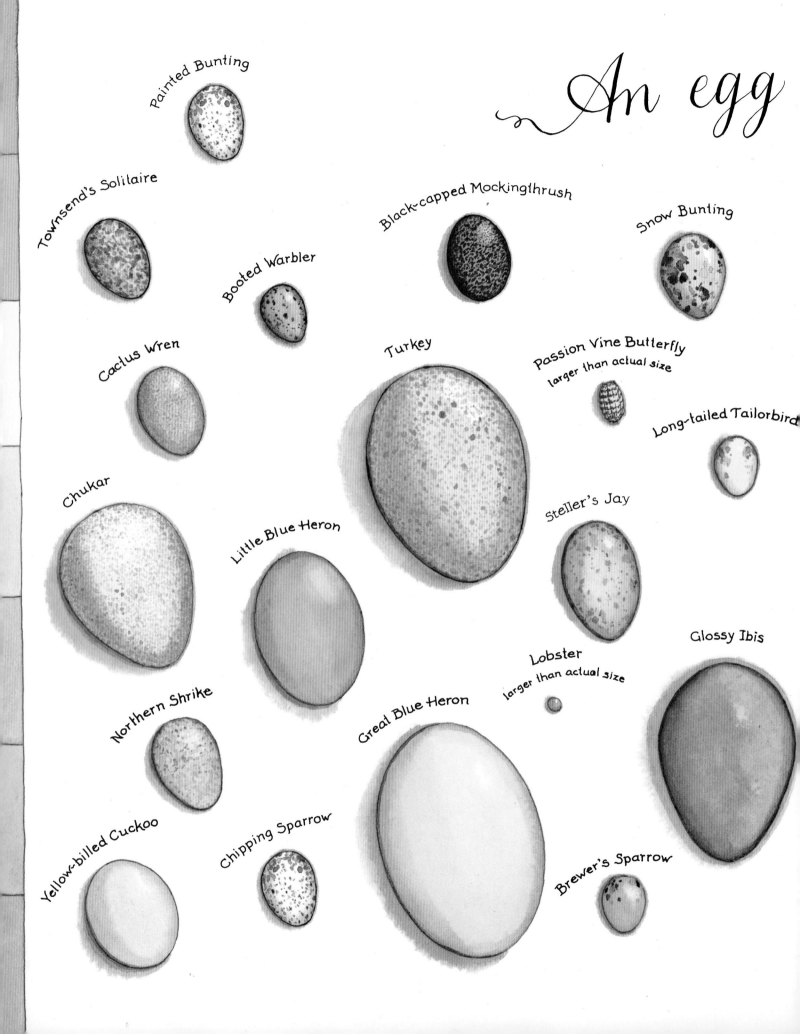

Painted Bunting

Townsend's Solitaire

Black-capped Mockingthrush

Snow Bunting

Booted Warbler

Cactus Wren

Turkey

Passion Vine Butterfly
larger than actual size

Long-tailed Tailorbird

Chukar

Little Blue Heron

Steller's Jay

Glossy Ibis

Lobster
larger than actual size

Northern Shrike

Great Blue Heron

Yellow-billed Cuckoo

Chipping Sparrow

Brewer's Sparrow

An egg

is colorful.

Fork-tailed Storm-petrel
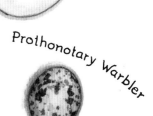

Black-naped Oriole

Bushy-crested Jay

King Salmon

Prothonotary Warbler

Thick-billed Warbler

Blue Crab

Kirtland's Warbler

Streaked Bittern

Herring Gull

Golden-crowned Kinglet

Field Cricket

Blue Jay

Hawfinch

Elegant Tinamou
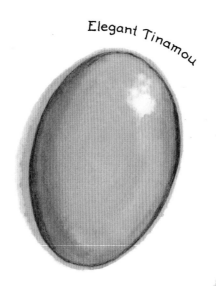

American Robin

California Thrasher
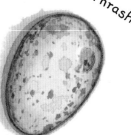

Hepatic Tanager

Gray Catbird

There are round eggs.

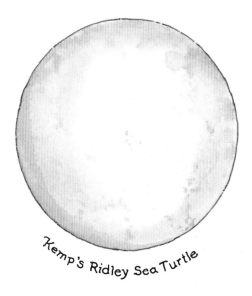

Kemp's Ridley Sea Turtle

Sea turtles dig a hole in the sand with their flippers and lay up to 200 soft, round eggs. Round eggs fit together nicely in tight spaces.

There are oval eggs.

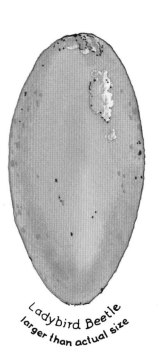

Ladybird Beetle
larger than actual size

When ladybugs hatch as larvae, their first meal is often the egg case they crawled out of.

is shapely.

There are even tubular eggs.

There are pointy eggs.

Common Murre

Dogfish

While most sharks give birth
to live young, some sharks,
like the lesser-spotted dogfish, begin
life in a leathery egg case with
tendrils. The tendrils anchor the eggs
to seaweed so they won't be
swept away by the ocean current.

Seabird eggs are pointy at
one end, so if they're laid on rock
ledges, they roll around in
safe little circles, not off the cliff.

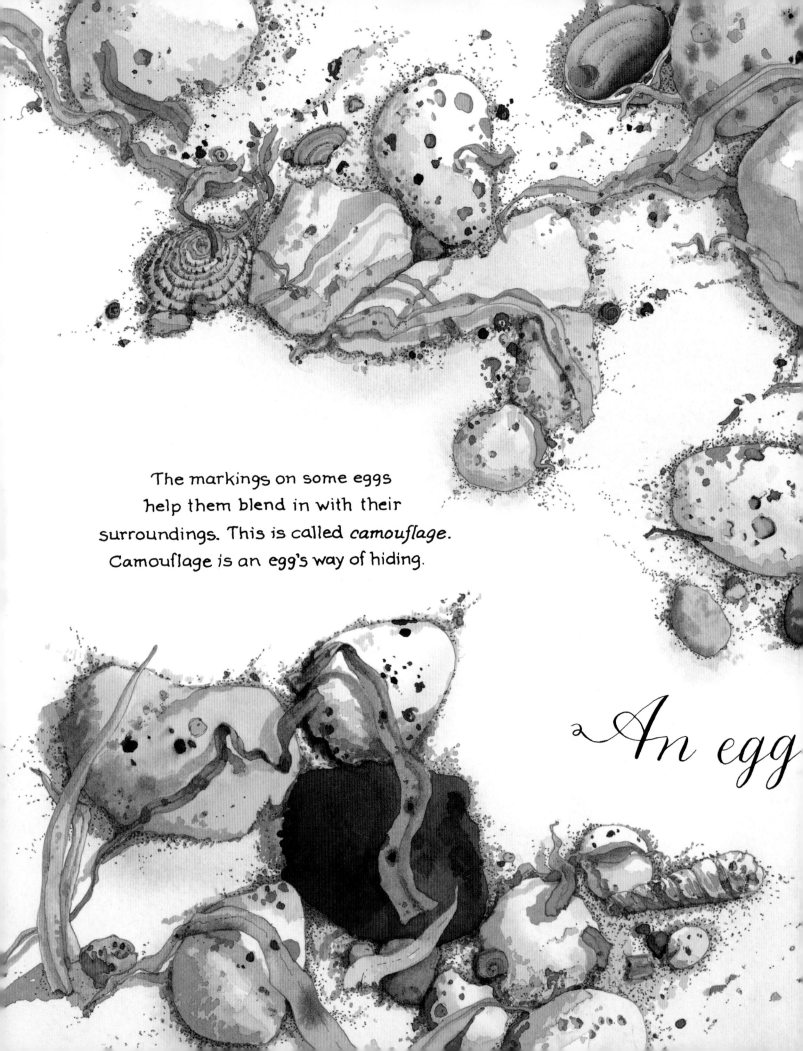

The markings on some eggs
help them blend in with their
surroundings. This is called *camouflage*.
Camouflage is an egg's way of hiding.

An egg

Sooty Tern

is clever.

An egg might be speckled to
resemble the rocks around it. Or it
might be gray, the color of mud by a lake.
An egg does not want to be eaten by
a raccoon or a snake or a fox or an insect.

Ostrich

An ostrich egg can weigh as much
as 8 pounds. It is so big and so round,
it takes two hands to hold one egg.

Eggs come in different sizes.

Anna's Hummingbird

Hummingbird eggs are the size of a jelly bean. It would take about 2,000 hummingbird eggs to equal the size of one ostrich egg.

Paradise Crow

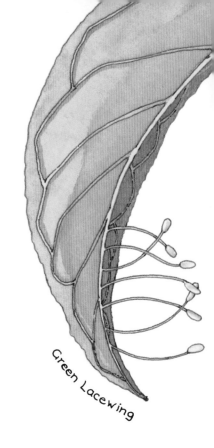
Green Lacewing

Yellowhammer

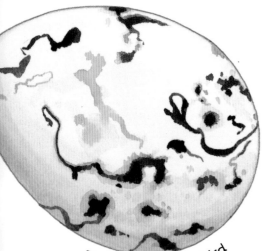
Red-winged Blackbird

An egg

Atlantic Salmon

Scarlet Tanager

Bronze-winged Jacana

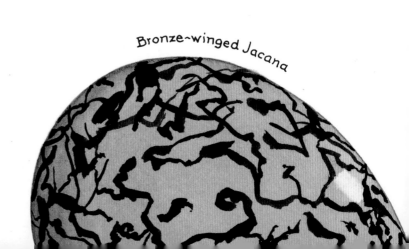

Paradise Riflebird

Arctic Tern

Evening Grosbeak

Sooty Tern

is artistic.

Katydid

Harlequin Bug

ggs on this page larger than actual size.

There are hard eggs

and gooey eggs.

and soft eggs

Boat-tailed Grackle

Bird eggs are hard.

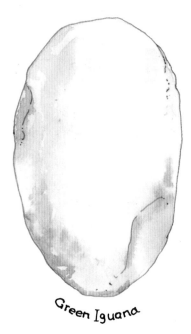

Green Iguana

Reptile eggs are often
soft and rubbery.

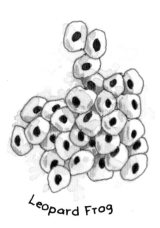

Leopard Frog

Amphibian eggs are gooey.
The "goo" keeps them from
drying out.

is textured.

and rough eggs.

There are smooth eggs

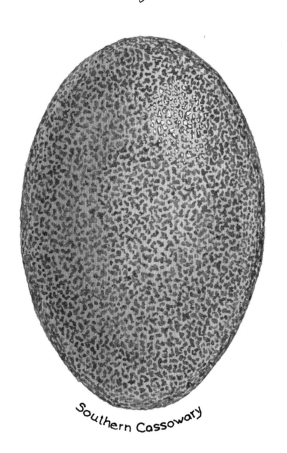

Southern Cassowary

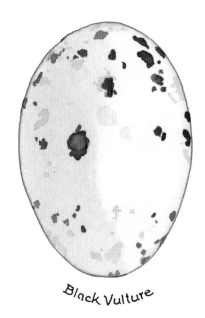

Black Vulture

Most bird eggs are smooth.

The eggs of cassowaries, emus, and cormorants are rough.

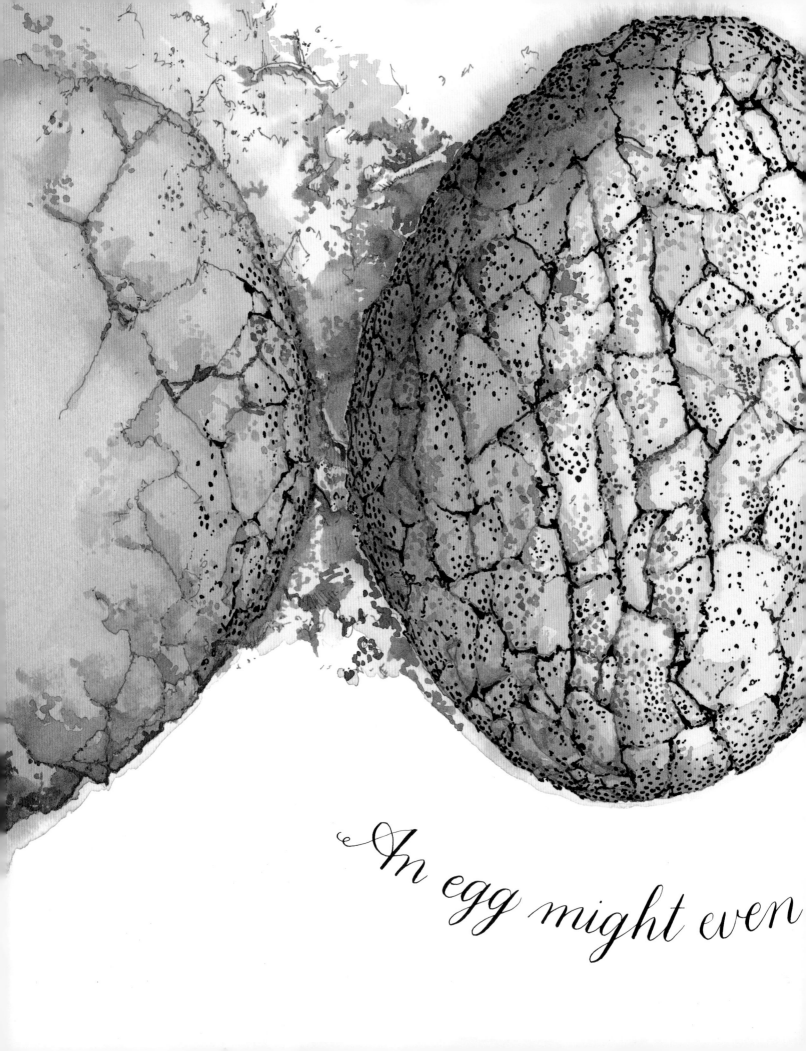

An egg might even

The remains of creatures that died millions of years ago may become rock-hard, or *fossilized*. Scientists have unearthed fossilized dinosaur eggs all around the world. Some are round, and some are oblong. Some are as small as one inch across, and some are as large as twenty inches. Scientists believe all dinosaurs hatched from eggs.

...be fossilized!

~An egg is giving.

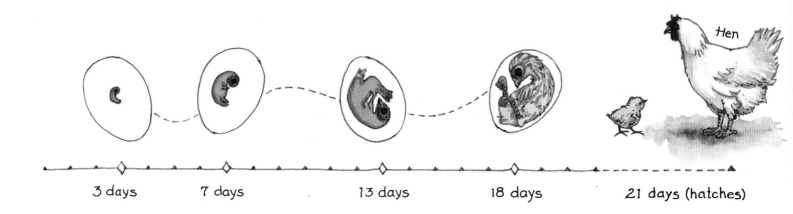

3 days   7 days   13 days   18 days   21 days (hatches)

Hen

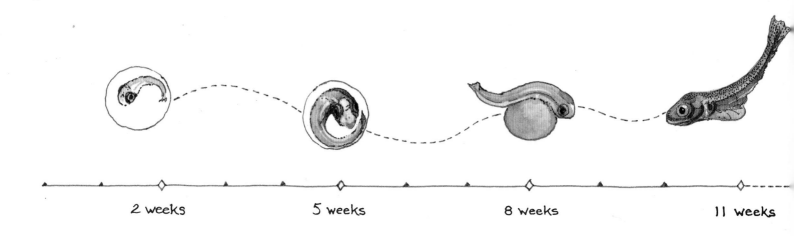

2 weeks   5 weeks   8 weeks   11 weeks

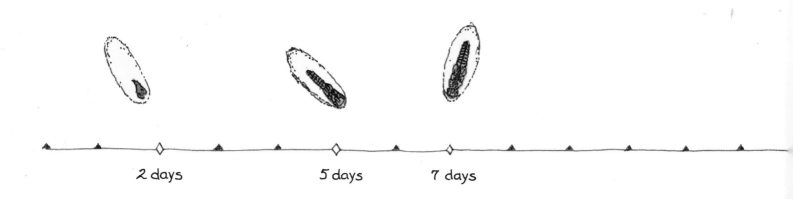

2 days   5 days   7 days

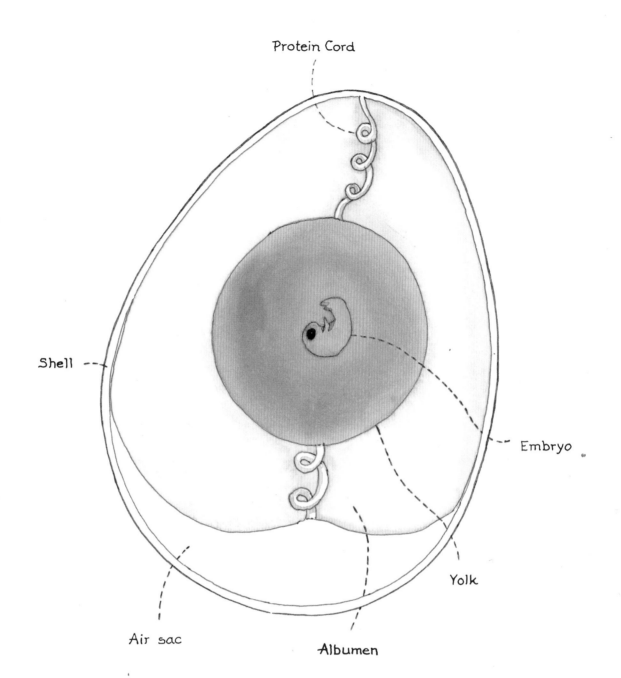

Protein Cord

Shell

Embryo

Yolk

Air sac

Albumen

Salmon

An egg gives the little creature growing
inside it everything it needs. The shell is its home.
The yolk is its food. The egg white, or albumen,
is its pillow. The shell is covered with
teeny tiny holes, which allow air to enter.

Grasshopper

15 days

A grasshopper embryo rests inside the egg
until the weather is just right.

An egg is quiet.

Then, suddenly . . .

Black-necked Stilt

an egg

crunch!

Green Vegetable Bug

cheep!

peep!

Black-necked Stilt Nestlings

is noisy!

crunch!

Passion Vine Caterpillar

cheep!

peep!

Paradise Riflebird

Passion Vine Butterfly

Steller's Jay

Lobster

Green Vegetable Bug

Fork-tailed Storm-petrel

Snow Bunting

Prothonotary Warbler

Elegant Tinam[ou]

Bushy-crested Jay

Common Murre

Northern Shrike

Blue Crab

Arctic Tern

Streaked Bittern

Herring Gull

California Thrasher

Katydid

Boat-tailed Grackle

Emperor Penguin

Kirtland's Warble[r]

Black Vulture

Cactus Wren

Hawfinch

Yellowhammer

Hepatic Tanager

Townsend's Solitaire

Blue Jay

Long-tailed Tailorbird

Harlequin Bug

Chukar

Anna's Hummingbird

Atlantic Salmon

Leopard Frog

Black-capped Mockingthrush

Bronze-winged Jacana

Red-winged Blackbird

Paradise Crow

Green Lacewing

Golden-crowned Kinglet

Scarlet Tanager

Glossy Ibis

Yellow-billed Cuckoo

Turkey

Black-necked Stilt

Little Blue Heron

Thick-billed Warbler

Sooty Tern

Brewer's Sparrow

Evening Grosbeak

Booted Warbler

Field Cricket

Gray Catbird

Black-naped Oriole

Chipping Sparrow

Dogfish

Green Iguana

American Robin

Ladybird Beetle

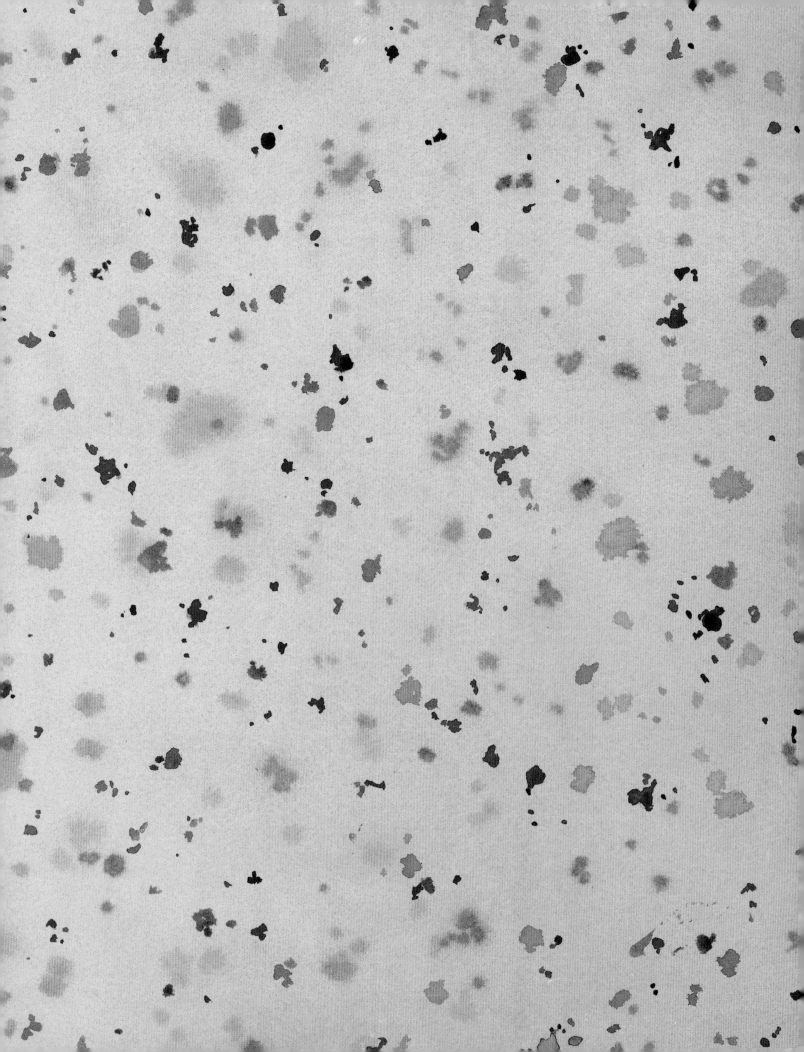